Song of Creation

Jennifer Minney

Silvertree

Published 2003
by
Silvertree Publishing
PO Box 2768, Yeovil, Somerset

ISBN: 0-9538446-1-7

A catalogue record for this book is available from the
British Library

Printed and bound by
Creeds the Printers, Broadoak, Bridport, Dorset DT6 5NL

Contents

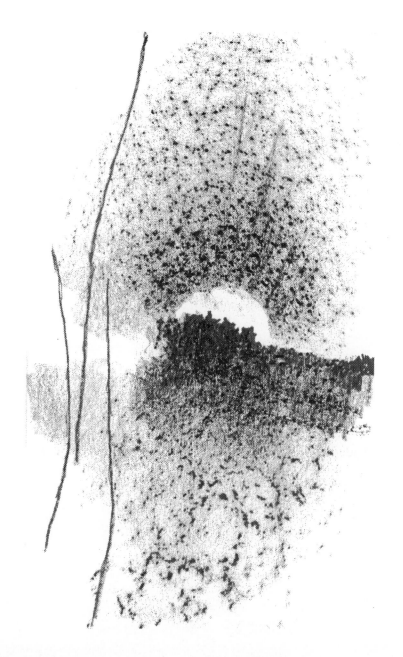

DAY 1

LIGHT AND DARKNESS

DAY AND NIGHT

In the beginning God created the heavens and the earth. Now the earth was formless and empty, darkness was over the surface of the deep, and the Spirit of God was hovering over the waters.

And God said, "Let there be light," and there was light. God saw that the light was good, and he separated the light from the darkness. God called the light "day", and the darkness he called "night". And there was evening, and there was morning — the first day. *(Genesis 1:1-5)*

IN THE BEGINNING

It is always dark
In the beginning.
It is always dark,
With senseless, vague alarm.
For thoughts conceived within the deep
Unconscious lie in troubled sleep
Before they make that dawning leap
To clarity and calm.

It is always dark
In the beginning.

There is never form
In the beginning.
There is never form:
No texture, colour, line.
But in that dark primordial night
New plans take shape and shimmer white
Before they surge towards the light
And burst with life divine.

There is never form
In the beginning.

O<>O<>O<>O<>O<>O<>O<>O

At the kingdom's dawn
An expensive tapestry
Woven from nothing.

LIVING LIGHT

World's beginning, planets spinning,
Suns colliding, moons dividing,
Stars exploding, earth encoding
Life that bursts with beauty bright:
Unimagined living light.

Noise and motion, sky and ocean
Pounding, pouring, raging, roaring;
Sweeping, surging, bright emerging
Life that throbs with awesome might:
Movement born of living light.

World's beginning, people sinning,
Life despoiling, troubled, toiling,
Hurting, hiding; God providing
Man's redemption, truth and right:
Life restored through Christ, the Light.

MORNING LIGHT AND EVENING

Morning light and evening,
Dawn and dusk enfolding,
Start and end of day.

Alpha and Omega,
Present, past and future,
Christ the Light, the Way.

Morning light and evening,
Life's first hopeful beaming,
Death's departing ray.

AND GOD MADE LIGHT

And God made light, with colours true,
The first-born three: red, yellow, blue.
From these a rich diversity
Existing from eternity.

Rosy dawn, the blush of day,
Poppies in a field of hay,
Crimson roses blooming fair,
Ruddy cheeks and Titian hair,
Glowing embers, burning fires,
Garnets, rubies, coral spires,
Russet apples, cherry cheer,
Robins, foxes, highland deer —
      Fiery red, a warming sight,
      And come to be when God made light.

Sunlight sparkling on the hills,
Primrose banks and daffodils,
Ripened barley, shimmering sand,
Gold and topaz, leather tanned,
Molten honey, butter, cheese,
Brimstone moths and brazen bees,
Hawks and eagles soaring high,
Harmless hamsters, tiger's eye —
      Earthy yellow, burnished might.
      O wondrous day when God made light!

Azure skies of summer dreams,
Cerulean lakes and streams,
Violets shy in garden plots,
Bluebell woods, forget-me-nots,
Beryl, turquoise, sapphire-glow,
Cobalt, woad and indigo,
Peacocks proud as Prussian kings,
Starlings' eggs and swallows' wings —
      Ocean blue, completing bright
      The primal three, when God made light.

WINDOW OF HEAVEN

From high above, the stained-glass light
Flung down a shaft of colour bright,
A beam of star-flecked sky
With swirling gems of dazzling flame
Cascading from a Gothic frame,
An endless, rich supply
Of emeralds, rubies, garnets, jade,
And sapphires blue in Heaven made.

And in the aisles, the dancing light
Formed patterns on the marble white,
An orbiting design
Of fiery gold and festive green,
An ever-changing sparkling scene
Imbued with life divine,
And touching soft the weary feet
Of worshippers, in blessing sweet.

And not content with this, the light
Surged upwards with prismatic might,
And splashed the sombre pews
With streaks of violet, orange, red,
And round the pillars boldly spread,
Proclaiming loud the news
That God, the light of lights, displays
His boundless love in countless ways.

0<>0<>0<>0<>0<>0<>0<>0<>0

From the source of life
Flowed forth a river of light,
And the darkness fled.

HOW LONG IS A DAY?

It's as long as a thought unravelled,
    and stretched from pole to pole.
It's as long as a road untravelled
    to an unimagined goal.

It's as long as a dream on waking,
    lost in a sleepy yawn.
It's as long as a thirst on slaking
    with the mountain dew of dawn.

It's as long as a pain unending,
    as long as a tear run dry.
It's as long as a heartache mending,
    and the echo of a sigh.

NIGHT TIME, DREAM TIME

Night time, dream time, when dormant thoughts awake
And start to stir in caverns underground;
Bubbling, boiling, churning up the lake
Of primal being, life's eternal round;
Thoughts inspired that, sheltered from the cold
Of conscious reason, thrive, shake off their mould
And greet the dawning day in shapes profound.

Night time, dream time, when fantasies arise
And soar across the mind's uncharted sea;
Leaping, lunging, driven by the sighs
Of ancient voices, breath of mystery;
Fantasies that, loosened from the chain
Of hardened logic, bring a fresh domain
To waking life: creative thought set free.

DARK NIGHT OF THE SOUL

Dark night of the soul,
When darkness, like a living thing —
A creature spawned from blackest hell —
Grabs hold with deadly tentacles,
Constricting, crushing, dragging down
To depths of dank despair.

Dark night of the soul,
When darkness, like a tidal wave —
A heaving mass of wailing wall —
Breaks down with force unstoppable,
Engulfing, swamping, drowning
In a stormy sea of tears.

Dark night of the soul,
When darkness, like a funeral garb —
A numbing, icy winding-sheet —
Wraps round its crippling bondages,
Compressing, squeezing, strangling life
With harbingers of death.

Dark night of the soul,
When darkness, like a heavy cloud —
A suffocating overlay —
Obscures the day, effectively
Destroying light, till all is dark.
And in the darkness, God.

0<>0<>0<>0<>0<>0<>0<>0

When the darkness comes
The light of the soul shines forth,
And sees more clearly.

WHERE LIGHT AND DARKNESS MEET

Deep In the silent shadowland,
Where day embraces darkest night,
The soul responds to gentle hand
That shields it from the searching light
Of zealous noon, its eager blaze.
The soul needs shade, and lowered gaze.

It's where the light and darkness meet,
And flickering shadows leap and loom,
The soul reveals in glimpses sweet
The secrets of its sacred womb.
The soul needs morning's misty grey
And gentle blush of dawning day.

Tread softly then, where memories sleep,
And thoughts lie curled in foetal dream,
And waken the unconscious deep
With tender touch and humbled gleam.
And hush. Be still. Make not a sound
As daylight breaks on hallowed ground.

O<>O<>O<>O<>O<>O<>O<>O

An ancient story
Buried beneath the ages
Of the human soul,
Waiting to be discovered
By the seeking eyes of love.

SONG OF CREATION

There's music in my heart —
music that wells within my breast
and echoes in my brain,
bringing me sweet, ecstatic pain.
It touches the depths of my soul
and tears me apart;
it also makes me whole.
And, oh, this music
hammering inside,
demanding to be expressed,
must stay imprisoned in my heart,
and only my eyes
that smart with unshed tears
show that there's music there.

There's music in my heart —
music that stirs unsounded depths
with words unspeakable
and feelings inexpressible.
And yet, at times it lifts me up
into a realm apart,
away from Earth's control,
and there I sit and laugh
at my escape.
And as my soul transcends
the barriers of this world,
the music of my soul
bursts forth and joins
the song of all creation.

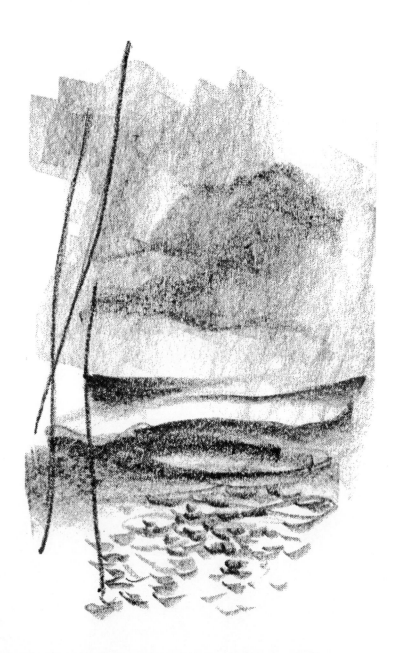

DAY 2

THE SKY AND SEA

And God said, "Let there be an expanse between the waters to separate water from water." So God made the expanse and separated the water under the expanse from the water above it. And it was so. God called the expanse "sky". And there was evening, and there was morning — the second day.   *(Genesis 1:6-8)*

EARTH WRAPPED IN WATER

Earth wrapped in water,
floating in water,
shrouded in gloom;
secretly forming,
growing and forming,
safe in God's womb.

New life created,
offspring created,
sprung from God's mind;
seeds of his loving,
father-like loving,
gentle and kind.

Earth wrapped in water,
breaking the water,
sky and the sea;
pushing through darkness,
splitting the darkness,
coming to be.

HOW DID THE WORLD BEGIN?

How did the world begin —
With a bang: a painful cry
Of sudden violent birth?
Or did it first, within
A watery womb of sea and sky,
Develop living earth,
Encoding slowly embryonic clay,
While waiting, eons-long, its natal day?

LIVING WATER

Living, loving, laughing water,
Bursting forth from God, his daughter:
Offspring of his love outflowing,
Shining, sparkling, glistening, glowing,
Surging through the barren earth,
Stirring life-forms, giving birth.

Gushing, gleaming, gurgling river,
Springing forth from God, the Giver.
Sister water, sweetly singing,
Music rising, rippling, ringing
Joyful through the hardened ground,
Filling Earth with living sound.

Rolling, roving, restless ocean,
By the Spirit's breath in motion;
Water swelling, swirling, streaming,
Spawning life abundant: teeming
Mass of beings, vast array
Greeting the primordial day.

0<>0<>0<>0<>0<>0<>0<>0<>0

In the beginning,
Lakes reflecting the heavens,
God's holy mirror
Showing a face of beauty,
Eyes full of infinite love.

SKY AND SEA

Waters above and waters below,
Life-giving water, life-stirring flow,
Washing the sky and preparing the earth
For seed-time and harvest, conception and birth;
Shining, refining, refreshing and sweet,
From God's holy mountain, his heavenly seat.

Waters above and waters below,
Mist and the rain and the soft fall of snow,
Forming the clouds from the dew on the ground,
Circling forever, around and around,
From blue sky above to the great salty sea,
And back to the heavens, abundant and free.

Waters below and waters above,
Borne on God's breath – Holy Spirit, sweet dove –
Blending with dust, forming life-teeming clay,
Bringing to being a new, perfect day.
Mystical water, a wonder untold,
Far brighter than silver, more precious than gold.

Waters below and waters above,
Gift of the Father, outpouring of love,
Gleaming and streaming from out and within,
Cleansing the soul from the dark stains of sin,
Healing, restoring, a blessing sublime,
And planned from the start, from the dawning of time.

O<>O<>O<>O<>O<>O<>O<>O<>O

Dew of the morning,
Tears of relief and laughter
Wept by the parched earth.

WAVES OF THOUGHT

Rushing thoughts upon the shore
Of consciousness, an endless tide
Of deep unrest, incessant roar
Of insights gleaned from far and wide:
Astounding, startling, untamed might,
Imploding, pounding, day and night.

Racing thoughts upon the sand
Of mortal time, converging streams
Of notions hard to understand;
Abstractions, theories, hopes and dreams
Dividing, splitting, circling round,
And plunging, puzzled, underground.

Settled thoughts in rocky pools,
Fast-held concepts, complex, deep;
Foolish wisdom, wit of fools,
Then, another tidal sweep:
Massing brain-waves, wild refrain
Stirring up the mind again.

TOUCH OF GOD

I sat alone, as day grew light,
And watched the clouds drift by,
And wavelets dancing, sparkling bright,
With rhythmic swish and sigh,
As white spume soared, unfettered, free,
Embracing soft the sand.
And lost in thought, beside the sea,
I felt my Father's hand.

WHAT IS SKY?

What is sky?

A canvas lovingly prepared
And washed with palest blue;
The ceiling of a chapel, aired
And fresh and rendered true;
A roof above a wondering world
For God to paint anew.

And what shall God, the Master, paint?
A big round sun of fiery red,
And clouds of soft-brushed white,
With gold and crimson deftly spread,
And arching rainbow bright,
Displaying bold the spectrum
Of his palette's prism-light.

And what is sky?

A curtain black, of rich brocade
With ordered stitching fine;
A cloak of velvet skilful made,
Of classic, noble line,
And plainly draped around the world,
Awaiting God's design.

And what shall God, the Craftsman, make?
A silver moon with cloudy haze,
A ruby planet, Mars,
A Venus-pearl with love ablaze,
And twinkling diamond stars:
Uncounted jewels shaped and set
In cosmic bright bazaars.

CLOUDS

Clouds like trailing spumes of smoke
    from a thousand chimney pots,
Making patterns high above,
    lines and circles, loops and knots.

Clouds like drifting eider down
    forming pillows soft and white,
Shaken by the bustling breeze,
    floating upward, feather-light.

Clouds like spreading ruby wine
    sweet from giant goblets spilt
On a cloth of fading blue,
    staining purple, edged with gilt.

Clouds like heavy blankets grey
    darkly wrapped around the sky,
Slowly changing, washed with rain
    and hung across the world to dry.

Clouds like flying sable cloaks
    worn by charging horsemen bold;
Wind-tossed mantles, lightning-fast,
    lined with satin silver-gold.

O<>O<>O<>O<>O<>O<>O<>O

Arching through the clouds,
A trellis made of sunshine
For growing raindrops.

SEA LONGING

Oh, take me back to the restless sea,
And the steep and stony shore,
Where the waves come riding wild and free,
With a rattle, hiss and roar,
And lines of breakers rush the bay,
And the rocks explode with foaming spray.

Oh, take me back to the open strand
Where the stiff sea breezes blow,
And the flying spume and the stinging sand
And the waters' ebb and flow,
Where winds come howling, furious, fast,
And whip the waves with frenzied blast.

Oh, take me back to the ocean wide,
And the bracing errant air,
Where the fresh sea-scent of the surging tide
Drowns every whiff of care,
And the tang of the deep and flowing brine
Restores the soul with a breath divine.

FLOATING

Floating on a timeless sea
Beneath a trackless sky,
Drifting through eternity,
Cushioned on a sigh,
As waves caress my drowsy form
And hush my fading ears,
And spray-kissed breezes, soft and warm,
Subdue my waking fears
As safe they close my eyes in sleep,
Rocked in the arms of the ocean deep.

BEYOND

O swirling vapours, clouds above,
My thoughts are swirling too,
And long to feel the push and shove
Of streaming winds with you.
I see your billows, dark with rain,
Expand and fill the sky,
While I'm held fast in Earth's domain,
My spirit wracked and dry.
But as I glimpse the truth of love
Beyond Earth's ages long,
I join with you, O clouds above,
In life's eternal song.

O raging ocean, restless sea,
My soul is restless too,
And longs to soar unfettered, free,
On white-spumed waves with you.
I see your billows pitch and roll
In endless, ceaseless round,
While I'm held fast in Earth's control,
My anxious spirit bound.
But as I grasp the power to be,
Beyond Earth's wide expanse,
I join with you, O restless sea,
In life's eternal dance.

O<>O<>O<>O<>O<>O<>O<>O

An endless river
Flowing from Heaven's mountain
To the timeless sea,
Quenching the spirit's longing
With a taste of things to come.

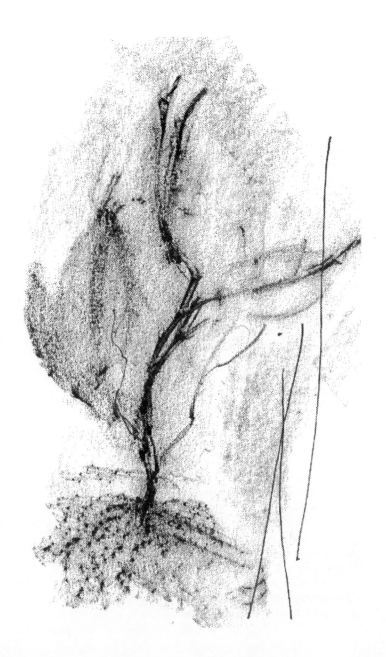

DAY 3

THE DRY GROUND

PLANTS AND TREES

And God said, "Let the water under the sky be gathered to one place, and let dry ground appear." And it was so. God called the dry ground "land", and the gathered waters he called "seas". And God saw that it was good.

Then God said, "Let the land produce vegetation: seed-bearing plants and trees on the land that bear fruit with seed in it, according to their various kinds." And it was so.... And God saw that it was good. And there was evening, and there was morning — the third day. *(Genesis I:9-13)*

GOD IN CREATION

From the barren ground, a root
First conceived within God's mind,
Growing green, a tender shoot
Made to reproduce its kind.

Life abundant bursting forth
Over valley, hill and plain,
East to west, and south to north,
Flowers and fruit and golden grain.

Staff of life, the ripening corn,
Joy of life, the reddening vine,
From the day that Earth was born,
Christ, our offering, bread and wine.

SOMETHING MORE

When I see the wandering clouds,
And mountains wrapped in snowy shrouds,
The forests wide with ancient trees,
And cornfields waving in the breeze,
The restless sea and sandy shore,
I know that there is something more
Than this, the world we see and feel;
There's something grander far, more real.
And then my searching soul transcends
The boundaries of this world, and blends
With fire and earth, the sky and sea,
To touch the great Eternity.

GOD REVEALED

In every forest, fen and field,
On windswept moor, on heath and weald,
There God in his creation is revealed.

In river, lake and waterfall,
In rocks and ridges, great and small,
There God is seen, the Maker of them all.

In oceans deep, in clouds and sky,
In valleys steep and mountains high,
There God appears to every seeing eye.

In sparkling stream, in babbling brook,
In dappled dell and shady nook,
There God is found by those who stop to look.

In every tree, in every leaf,
In flower and herb and harvest sheaf,
There God is shown, our Lord and sovereign Chief.

In all God's wondrous works we see
The imprint of the Trinity:
The Father, Son and Spirit, one in three.

God's Spirit reaches everywhere,
And shines through each creation fair.
Where beauty, love and truth are, God is there.

0<>0<>0<>0<>0<>0<>0<>0

A rippling river,
Unable to keep silent,
Singing a love song.

WATCHING

Watching the cloudy billows
and the lazy drifts of vapour
forming slowly moving patterns
in the never-ending sky;
tumbled beds of softness,
mounds of downy whiteness,
for dreams to snuggle into,
as gentle as a sigh.

Watching the raindrops falling:
orbs of crystal water
spreading ever-widening circles
on the shining, silver lake;
ruffled rounds of laughter,
rippling arms of rapture,
dispelling gloomy musings
and hugging hope awake.

Watching the daylight dancing:
darting gleams of glory
leaving fairy-trails of wonder
on the fields of ripened hay;
endless golden carpet
of sparkling, spangled beauty
for weary thoughts to walk on,
and find a better way.

0<>0<>0<>0<>0<>0<>0<>0

A weeping willow
Looking at the bright river,
And finding comfort.

FOREST WHISPERS

My fingers touched the tree's rough bark,
And traced its ancient features, lined
And marked with etchings deep, and dark
As thoughts concealed from conscious mind;
Dark as the womb, its mother, earth,
That housed its seed and gave it birth.

And how my aching fingers craved
To touch its soul, those inner rings,
Wheels within wheels, cycles engraved
With Eddas of eternal springs;
To trace that mythic triune root
Back to the source of life's first shoot.

Then soft a breath of wind arose,
Rustling the branches high above,
Making them whisper Heaven knows
What tales of death, new life and love.
And through the breath that stirred the wood,
I sensed the truth, and understood.

GOD'S CATHEDRAL

Beechwood pillars graceful rise
in columns from the forest floor:
a rich mosaic of copper-red,
with amber, bronze and gleaming gold;
while arching emerald branches,
finely carved with foliage,
flicker bright as, from the squints
beneath the vaulted sky,
shafts of swirling pearly light
soft diffuse round altared mounds
in earthy incense air.

THE NORTHLAND

Bleak are the northern hills that raise
Their craggy heads to meet the clouds,
And rough the slopes with untrod ways
Enveloped in those misty shrouds.

Chill are the northern streams that flow
In gullies down those hills austere,
And chatter through the dales below,
Their voices rising loud and clear.

Wild are the northern dales that lie
Untamed between those lowering hills,
And sturdy are the shrubs that try
To bloom amid the rocks and rills.

Cold is the northern wind that howls
Unchecked across that harsh terrain,
Wrapping the peaks in snowy cowls
And blustering sheets of sleeting rain.

Bleak are the hills and chill the streams,
And wild the dales where cold winds blow,
But this, the landscape of my dreams,
Is one I love and cherish so.

O<>O<>O<>O<>O<>O<>O<>O

An impatient wind
Making an epic journey
Over land and sea,
Rushing to tell its story
To the eerie rocks and caves.

GREEN ARE THE HEDGEROWS

Green are the hedgerows, and fragrant with dew,
And scattered with colour, the pink, purple, blue
Of campion and cranesbill, and sweet lady's smock,
And violet and vetchling, with parsley and dock,
And bedstraw and bindweed, abundant supply;
Profusion of beauty, a feast for the eye.

And green are the meadows, with buttercups spread,
And daisies and clover, with pimpernel red,
And meadowsweet forming dense clusters of cream,
With bright ragged robin by river and stream,
And balsam and burnet, their heads lifted high;
Profusion of beauty, a feast for the eye.

And green are the mountains where rock roses bloom,
And pale purple heather, and sorrel and broom,
Where foxglove and bugle stand bold on the hills,
And hosts of bright gentian by steep running rills,
And blue Jacob's ladder, at one with the sky;
Profusion of beauty, a feast for the eye.

O<>O<>O<>O<>O<>O<>O<>O<>O

Crowds of celandine
Assembling by the pathway
To the new-crowned trees,
Waiting to pay their homage
In a burst of golden praise.

A BLUEBELL WOOD

One day, in sad and pensive mood,
    My thoughts began to stray,
And with my spirit's eyes I viewed
    A bluebell wood in May.

Beneath the leafy trees was spread
    A heavenly carpet new,
A dense, unending flower bed
    Of pale celestial blue.

On bending stems the clustered bells
    Swayed soundless in the breeze,
And filled the soft-lit hazy dells
    With quietness and ease.

And in my thoughts, I held my face
    Against those fragrant flowers,
Whose perfume, in a sweet embrace,
    Enveloped me for hours.

A LEAF

Deep in bluebell woods, a bridge,
Old and cobbled grey,
Crouches low across a racing stream;
And there in carefree childhood days
Long past, I used to play;
Standing on its bending back
To launch my leaf with artless throw,
And watch it sail away,
Applauded by the spruce and larch,
Triumphal through the low grey arch.

DANDELION DOUBTS

One day, while walking sad and slow
Through fields where dandelions grow,
I plucked a fluffy flower to blow.
He loves me.

But then, I thought, it seems today
That God is very far away,
And doesn't hear me when I pray.
He loves me not.

Yet deep within my heart I knew
That God is faithful, loving, true,
And does just what he says he'll do.
He loves me.

But as I focused on my pain,
And thought of how I'd prayed in vain,
I started doubting him again.
He loves me not.

At last, I looked toward the sky,
And watched the pollen floating high,
Convinced that God can never lie.
He loves me.

0<>0<>0<>0<>0<>0<>0<>0

Golden buttercups
Embroidered on God's footstool,
Adorning the Earth.

DAY 4

THE SUN, MOON AND STARS

THE SEASONS

And God said, "Let there be lights in the expanse of the sky to separate the day from the night, and let them serve as signs to mark seasons and days and years, and let them be lights in the expanse of the sky to give light on the earth." And it was so. God made two great lights — the greater light to govern the day and the lesser light to govern the night. He also made the stars. God set them in the expanse of the sky to give light on the earth, to govern the day and the night, and to separate light from darkness. And God saw that it was good. And there was evening, and there was morning — the fourth day.   *(Genesis 1:14-19)*

BROTHER SUN

Brother sun, let us greet together
the dawning day,
creation's new beginning.
Let us warm together
with holy fire
the hearts of all things living.
Let us join together
in joyful praise
of God, our great Creator.
Let us bless each other in love.
Brother sun, I love you.

Sister moon, let us light together
the dreary night,
God's greater light reflecting.
Let us smile together
through mist and cloud,
through waxing pale and waning.
Let us join together
in joyful praise
of God, our great Creator.
Let us bless each other in love.
Sister moon, I love you.

Sister stars, let us dance together
and fill the heavens
with movement, bright and sparkling.
Let us sing together
of Earth's first morn:
a hymn of celebrating.
Let us join together
in joyful praise
of God, our great Creator.
Let us bless each other in love.
Sister stars, I love you.

THE MOON

Daughter of night, sweet woman of mystery,
Softly reflecting the sun's brighter glow,
Shrouded in mistiness, shining and silvery,
Smiling serenely at darkness below.

Daughter of night, sweet woman of mystery,
Wispily wrapped in a gossamer veil,
Peeping through cloudiness, eyes soft and fluttery,
Showing in glimpses your beauty so pale.

Daughter of night, sweet woman of mystery,
Beaming with happiness far out in space,
Joined by your sisters, the stars of the galaxy,
Showing uncovered your radiant face.

Daughter of night, sweet woman of mystery,
Racing through clouds on a wild, stormy night,
Boldly revealing, in moments of ecstasy,
All your white nakedness, shimmering bright.

MORNING STARS

Were you there when the stars sang
Together, and the heavens rang
With the music of the galaxy?
Were you there when the stars sang
Together, and the heavens rang
With joy — a glorious symphony
Of worship, an exploding air
Of praise and adoration? Were you there?

A DAY IN THE FOREST

Morning in the forest, and the sun,
Appearing through the branches, sheds
A pearly light: a radiance spun
From dewdrops on the sleepy heads
Of birch and ash, that with the mist
Disperse, remaining only deep
In shady groves; while on the sun-kissed
Grass the shadows homeward creep.

Midday in the forest, and the breeze
Begins to dance in merry mime
With dappled leaves that taunt and tease
In spot-lit shades of startling lime;
While soaring upwards, heaven high,
The sun imparts an emerald sheen
On stippled tree trunks, cracked and dry,
And paints the grass a dazzling green.

Evening in the forest, and the light
Is softly filtered through a veil
Of fine-spun gold, and tinges bright
The leaves embossed upon a pale
Blue sky; while tangled branches stark
Embrace the setting sun, then blend
With slowly greying trunks as dark
The shadows meet at daylight's end.

Night time in the forest, and the moon
With silver fingers starts to trace
A pattern on the bark, and soon
Drapes soft the trees in shining lace —
A work of wonder, braiding fine
With scattered sequins: stars above —
While, rising through the jagged line
Of pine trees, Venus beams her love.

THE SEASONS' ROUND

Springtime, and the promise bright
Of heather on the hills,
And cloudlets drifting, feather-light,
And sparkling rocks and rills;
The trees on bud, and snowdrops white,
With violets shy a welcome sight,
And smiling daffodils.

Summer, and a shimmering haze
Between the earth and sky,
And golden beaches, lazy days,
And meadows green and dry;
When roses bloom and gardens blaze
With flowers that warmly meet the gaze
Of shady trees grown high.

Autumn, and the rain's soft beat
On drifts of fallen leaves,
The smell of orchards, apple-sweet,
And vines and new-thatched eaves;
A mellow sun come out to greet
The ripened fields of waving wheat,
And bless the harvest sheaves.

Winter, and the trees stripped bare
As cold the north winds blow,
And stubbled fields that bravely wear
Their shifts of glistening snow;
A sombre sky, the sun's pale glare,
And yuletide logs with festive fare,
And wreaths of mistletoe.

SPRING

When, from the hard and hoary winter ground,
The snowdrops thrust their pale beribboned heads,
And crocuses in purple drifts abound,
And tulips fill the empty flowerbeds;
When trees that through the long, hard winter stood
Devoid of leaf, their branches numbly bare,
Begin at last to burst with ripening bud,
And perfume sweet of blossom fills the air;
When, on the snowy hilltops bleak and cold,
New grass springs up, and white is turned to green,
When slopes are freshly clad in gorse-rich gold,
And heather bright reforms the sombre scene;
    When all of nature wakes to life anew,
     0 Lord, I give all thanks and praise to you.

I DREAMED THAT IT WAS SUMMER

I dreamed that it was summer
        in a garden bright and fair,
And the flowers, ablaze with colour,
        caught the sun's unclouded glare,
With the rock plants, ferns and grasses,
        crimson roses climbing high,
And uncounted shrubs in blossom
        reaching up to touch the sky.
Their intoxicating perfume
        filled the sultry summer air,
And no blight destroyed the beauty
        of that garden bright and fair.

I dreamed that it was summer
      on an island in the sea,
And the sand was warm, embracing,
      and the rivers running free;
And the orchids, wild, exotic,
      splashed with flame the rocky bays,
While the palms held up their branches
      to the sun's enticing rays,
And the smell of peach and mango
      filled each valley, hill and lea,
And no coldness marred the beauty
      of that island in the sea.

I dreamed that it was summer
      on a hillside far away,
And the sunlight sparkled golden
      on the fields of ripening hay,
While the poppies, red and vibrant,
      lined the hedgerows in the glade,
And the trees in full-leaved glory
      spread their welcome dappled shade.
The grass smelled sweet and fragrant
      through the long luxuriant day,
And the sun shone bright forever
      on that hillside far away.

0<>0<>0<>0<>0<>0<>0<>0

Warm sand embracing,
The sea singing a love song,
And the sun's hot kiss.

AUTUMN

Autumn fulfilling hopes of spring,
When ripened lines of golden corn
Rise up to greet the harvest morn,
And meet the scythe's embracing swing;

When generous fruit trees proudly bear
On bending boughs their produce sweet,
And offer them at Heaven's feet,
The rosy apple, plum and pear;

When softly through the mellow days
The blushing vines their gifts bestow,
And fields with bounty overflow,
And all the Earth gives thanks and praise.

AFTER THE HARVEST

When the harvest's gathered in,
and hayricks dot the empty fields,
what joy to then behold
the golden autumn evening
spread a mantle soft and warm.

And what delight to see
on stubbled meadows, strangely bare,
a quilt of patchwork light,
woven by the laughing sun
on looms of scudding clouds.

THE WINTER WOOD

A twig snapped, piercing the silence of the wood,
That in the dawn stood cold and still as death.
I stopped, afraid to move, and spellbound stood,
Watching the icy vapour of my breath,
And wondering what it was that held me back
From crunching through the freshly-fallen snow
That carpeted the winding woodland track,
And sparkled in the pale sun's wintry glow.

No trees moved. Did they too feel the cloistered calm
And frozen stand, in shrouded winter rest?
No wailing wind disturbed the healing balm.
No rushing fool or uninvited guest
Came barging in to rend the air with sound
Or mar with careless tread the mystic rood.
And I turned back, for this was holy ground —
A haven. And I could not there intrude.

SPRING PROMISE

I saw a tree on bud today,
And snowdrops clustered white,
And though the sky was leaden grey,
My heavy heart grew light.
For after winter cold and drear,
And nights so dark and long,
What else the spirit sad can cheer
And lift it with a song,
But signs of spring? O, welcome spring,
A breath of life anew
That sweetly touches everything,
And brings a promise true.

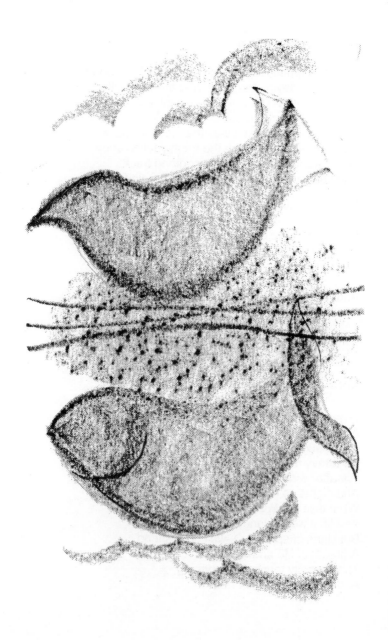

DAY 5

SEA CREATURES AND BIRDS

And God said, "Let the water teem with living creatures, and let birds fly above the earth across the expanse of the sky." So God created the great creatures of the sea and every living and moving thing with which the water teems, according to their kinds, and every winged bird according to its kind. And God saw that it was good. God blessed them and said, "Be fruitful and increase in number and fill the water in the seas, and let the birds increase on the earth." And there was evening, and there was morning — the fifth day.   *(Genesis 1:20-23)*

FUN FISHES

Fishes in perpetual motion
Flitting through the emerald ocean,
Frothy as a fairy potion,
Fickle, fey and fine.

Spotted, speckled, striped and stippled,
Banded, brindled, ribbed and rippled,
Marbled, mottled, tangled, tippled:
Flushed with coral wine.

Silver-grey and golden gleaming,
Pearl and amber, brightly beaming,
Jasper, jade, translucent, teeming
Gems of rare design.

Sapphire blue and rich rubescent,
Topaz, turquoise, iridescent,
Gaudy as a Christmas present
Tied with rainbow twine.

Dancing, dazzling, darting, dashing,
Glinting, glowing, flaming, flashing,
Fins a-flicking, tails a-lashing
Through the sparkling brine.

Fishes in perpetual motion
Flitting through the emerald ocean,
Frothy as a fairy potion,
Fickle, fey and fine.

THE SALMON

Beside a weary road, one day,
     I saw a river wide
Rush headlong down towards the bay,
A swelling stream with flying spray,
     Tormented by the tide.

And there I stopped, with troubled frown,
     And watched a waterfall:
A cataract of great renown
With raging torrents crashing down
     On boulders great and small.

And then, with sudden quickening cheer,
     I saw the salmon leap.
Abandoning their comfort sphere,
They hurtled from the water clear
     To scale the rapids steep.

And time again, with feelings stirred,
     I saw the salmon fail,
But keep on trying undeterred,
In spite of hope so oft deferred,
     Until they could prevail.

And on that long and weary road,
     I thought with praise of him:
The Ichthus, sign and secret code
Of those who, leaving safe abode,
     Against the current swim.

INSECT LIFE

There's a stirring in the water,
There's a whirring in the air,
There's a creeping and a crawling,
And a glimmer, gleam and glare;
There's a tunnelling and tapping
With a heaving of the earth,
And a fluttering and flapping
As the insects come to birth.

There's a happy honey humming
With the birthing of the bees,
And a twisting and a turning
Of the praying mantises;
There's a milling of mosquitoes
And a hovering of flies,
And consuming clouds of locusts
Rising up to fill the skies.

There are beetles, bugs, and bristletails,
And silverfish and lice;
There are fireflies sending signals
With their mating-light device;
There are earwigs, wasps and weevils,
An encroaching cockroach mass,
Insects stick-like on the branches,
Chirping crickets in the grass.

There are dragonflies and damselflies,
On ponds a dazzling sight;
There are stoneflies, thrips and scorpion flies,
And lacewings fairy-light;
There are ants and teeming termites,
Jumping fleas, of dubious worth,
And a bevy bright of butterflies
As insects come to birth.

THE BUTTERFLY

I stood and watched a butterfly
That fluttered by my door:
A Cabbage White, and one that I
Had often seen before.
And, since she was a common sight,
I'd never in the past
Observed how delicate and light
Her markings. But, at last,
I noticed just how soft and fine
Her fragile wings, and fey,
And saw the intricate design
Of black and palest grey
That marked their tips: a lovely hue
That matched her tiny head
And slender body, feelers too,
Each one a silken thread.
And as the little butterfly
Went fluttering by my door,
I couldn't help but wonder why
I'd seen her not before.

TO A CATERPILLAR

Caterpillar on a leaf,
Although it seems beyond belief,
One day you will fly.
You'll soar on painted lady wings,
And dance in tawny-orange rings
Against an azure sky.
So as you munch your thistle leaf,
Cling firmly to the sound belief
That one day you will fly.

BIRDS

Filling the heavens, they rise on the wing,
Spirits as light as the air;
Feathered, unfettered, they joyfully sing,
Extolling the freedom they share.

Soaring up mountains with powerful beat,
Over the ice and the snow;
Gliding through valleys where bright rivers meet
Like ribbons of silk far below.

Crossing the oceans and watching the play
Of billows, where sea horses ride;
Smelling the brine and the white salty spray,
Racing the fast-running tide.

Skimming through woodlands and meadows and leas,
Chasing the sun's darting beams;
Flapping and fluttering in bushes and trees,
Swooping on chattering streams.

Filling the heavens, they rise on the wing,
Spirits as light as the air;
Feathered, unfettered, no wonder they sing,
Extolling the freedom they share.

O<>O<>O<>O<>O<>O<>O<>O<>O

A white owl watching
The moon's reflection dancing
On a silver stage.

TO A BLACKBIRD

Of what do you sing, blithe blackbird?
Do you sing of the sky above,
And white clouds drifting, soft as down,
And nestling mother-love?
Do you sing of the dawn and morning light,
And the thrill of your soaring fledgling flight?

Of what do you sing, blithe blackbird?
Do you sing of the branching trees,
And green leaves rustling, soothing-sweet,
And the gentle zephyr breeze?
Do you sing of the ferns and flowers fair,
And the cooling rush of the scented air?

Of what do you sing, blithe blackbird?
Do you sing of the meadows wide,
And the green grass springing, dewy bright,
And the purple mountainside?
Do you sing of the rocks and rippling streams,
And hidden vales and secret dreams?

O<>O<>O<>O<>O<>O<>O<>O

The moon's rays piercing
The blue apple left behind,
A blackbird swooping
Down to sleep, a hyacinth
Smiling in the sapphire snow.

THE SPARROW

Great poets praise the eagle
For his soaring strength in flight,
The peacock for his colours,
Or the swan for plumage white,
The swallow for his gracefulness,
The hawk for vision clear,
The nightingale for music sweet,
The robin for his cheer.
To birds like these the poets write,
And songs of worship raise,
But rate the little sparrow
As unworthy of their praise.

How sad that any writer
Should ignore this little bird,
Whose voice above the roar
Of urban traffic can be heard.
For dull would be the city streets
If he should fly away,
And sing no more his chirpy song
To brighten up the day.
Perhaps, compared with other birds,
He is the least of all.
But God sees every sparrow
On the street unnoticed fall.

O<>O<>O<>O<>O<>O<>O<>O

Birds and butterflies,
Wings flashing in the sunlight:
Handfuls of colour
Flung against a blue canvas
By an exuberant God.

WILD GOOSE

Wild goose, wild goose, soaring high,
Circling in the darkening sky,
Let me join your noisy throng,
For my heart is stirred by your wild-goose song
And the rhythmic beat of your shining wings
As you swoop and swirl in moonlit rings,
Awaiting that signal, soft as sighs,
When in whirls of white as one you'll rise
And head for that country bright and fair,
Where the wind blows fresh and scents the air
With fragrant pine as dawn awakes
The primal forests, fields and lakes.
Oh, wild goose, wild goose, hear me pray.
Please take me with you, far away.

FIREBIRD

Firebird, perishing in flame,
Huddled in your bitter nest
Of myrrh and frankincense, your name
Lives on as, from the west
Towards the sun, your offspring flies,
On phoenix blood and body fed;
For as the offering burning dies,
New life springs up in fiery red.

Firebird, soaring to the sun,
From whence arose your mythic song:
The tale of death and life begun
That echoes through the ages long?
What distant lakes of briny fires
And hidden isles of breeding rings
Gave rise to fabled funeral pyres
And clouds of flaming fledgling wings?

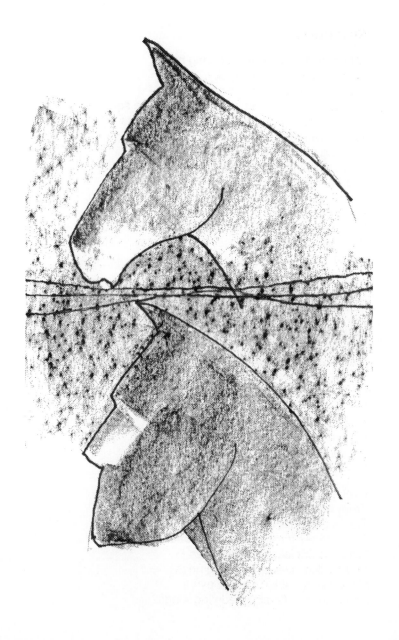

DAY 6

ANIMALS AND MAN

And God said, "Let the land produce living creatures according to their kinds: livestock, creatures that move along the ground, and wild animals, each according to its kind." And it was so.... And God saw that it was good.

Then God said, "Let us make man in our image, in our likeness, and let them rule over the fish of the sea and the birds of the air, over the livestock, over all the earth, and over all the creatures that move along the ground."

So God created man
    in his own image,
in the image of God
    he created him;
male and female
    he created them.

God saw all that he had made, and it was very good. And there was evening, and there was morning — the sixth day.   *(Genesis I:24-27, 31)*

THE LION AND THE LAMB

The lion, in his majesty and pride,
Beside the little lamb shall peaceful lie;
The hunter and the hunted side by side,
The fearsome meeting calm the fearful eye.
But where shall nestle warm the lion's mane
Against the lamb's soft coat of woolly white?
Shall they from high survey a sweeping plain
Of Africa in starry velvet night?
Or shall they in an English meadow view
The budding trees, the flowering shrubs of spring,
Lying in grass made fragrant with the dew
Of misty morning, sharing a daisy ring?
       The two in one, the fire and sacrifice,
       Symbols of Christ, redemption, paradise.

FAIR GAZELLE

Upon the hills of Judah,
     in open fields you dwell,
A creature formed in beauty,
     God's favoured – fair gazelle.
With eyes so soft and gentle,
     your kingdom you survey.
You watch until the daybreak,
     and the shadows flee away.

You leap upon the mountains,
     you roam through vale and dell,
You browse among the lilies,
     God's favoured – fair gazelle.
Your name means love and beauty,
     and so I ask you, "Stay.
Remain with me forever,
     till the shadows flee away."

MOORLAND PONY

Moorland pony, roaming free,
Wandering far and wide,
Sniffing the scent of the far-off sea,
And galloping with the tide,
The fragrant earth beneath your feet,
And the heather, gorse, and grasses sweet.

Moorland pony, roaming wild
Under the open sky,
By rocky streams where, undefiled,
The ancient stones stand high;
Where winds blow fresh, the sun shines bright,
And stars, unhindered, bless the night.

THE FEARFUL MOLE

One summer, I was sitting in my tent
When, from the ground, up popped a little mole.
Surprised, he looked around, and then he went
Back underground, into his little hole.

I wondered why he didn't choose to stay
Above the ground, beneath a sky of blue,
And take advantage of the light of day
To go exploring, finding life anew.

Perhaps he felt afraid and insecure
In this exciting world, poor little mole,
Preferring a restricted life, but sure,
And needing the protection of his hole.

ADAM

Adam, in your brand new garden,
Did you gaze at God's creation,
Full of awe and startled wonder,
Touch the flowers and thoughtful ponder,
Count their colours, feel their vibrance,
Deep inhale their heady fragrance,
Press your face into their beauty,
Name them as befit their beauty,
At the dawn of time?

Did you smile as bending branches
Formed above you emerald arches,
Watch the leaves, their fairy fluttering,
Hush to hear their rhythmic rustling,
Try to catch the sunbeams streaking,
Play with shadows hide and seeking,
Trace the pillars' mystic markings,
Name the trees to suit their markings,
At the dawn of time?

Did you see a streamlet rushing
Down the hillside, gurgling, gushing,
Marvel at its rapid movement,
Revel in its frothy ferment,
Gasp to feel its startling wetness,
Laugh to taste its icy sweetness,
Listen to its lively chatter,
Name it for its lively chatter,
At the dawn of time?

Did you run beside a river
Where the waters shake and quiver,
Throw some pebbles, watch them skimming,
See the little fishes swimming,
Join their crazy zig-zag races,
Laughing at their comic faces,

Try to catch their dappled brightness,
Name them for their dappled brightness,
At the dawn of time?

Did you lie on hillsides dreaming,
Watching birds at sunrise streaming,
Gasp to see them soaring, gliding,
Circling round and fearless diving,
Thrill to hear the woodlands ringing
With their sweet ecstatic singing,
Marvel at their feathered splendour,
Name the birds to match their splendour,
At the dawn of time?

Did you romp with living creatures,
Chuckling at their furry features,
Hold your cheek against their softness,
Wrap your arms around their sleekness,
Laugh to see them crawling, creeping,
Prowling, prancing, lunging, leaping,
Wonder at their power and purpose,
Name them as befit their purpose,
At the dawn of time?

Adam, in your brand new garden,
Did you see the moon's reflection
Through the trees on wavelets dancing
In a mirror-lake entrancing?
Did you, under God's bright heaven,
Smile in joyful recognition
Of yourself and Eve, the woman?
Was it there you named the woman,
At the dawn of time?

A CHILD IS...

A joy, a pain, life's worst and best,
An angel fair, a little pest;
A scruffy urchin, model neat,
A ball of rage, a bundle sweet;
A noise machine, a melody,
An open book, a mystery;
A joke, a puzzle, clown, a quirk,
A lot of fun, a lot of work;
The cause of laughs, the source of tears,
A comfort in the passing years;
A spreading branch, a blossom rare,
A jewel bright beyond compare;
A wonder sent from Heaven above,
A precious gift of life and love.

GRANNA DAVO

I used to find her, when she lived nearby,
 Creating dreams from scraps of cloth and thread,
Her song raised with the Singer's, pepper head
Sharp bowed; or up a ladder, eagle eye
Alight, forming an open, flowery sky
On cramped, damp ceilings, colours boldly spread;
Or stirring bubbling broth, or pounding red
Her foaming wash, and dancing rainbows dry.

I saw her last – I caught her unawares –
Perched upright on a makeshift bed: two chairs
Beneath the window where, with gaze intent,
She viewed the narrow street and far-off lands,
And munched with toughened gums her bread content,
While plucking grubby sheets with work-worn hands.

SPANISH LADY

A little lady, swathed in black,
Sat pensive in the Spanish sun,
Her face deep-lined, each wrinkled track
An ancient tale of battles won,
Of passions spent and worn-out pain,
Of love and loss, and hard-earned gain.

A little lady, huddled low
Upon her doorstep dusty-grey,
Sat silent as an endless flow
Of noisy tourists passed her way.
She watched unmoved the changing scene,
Her gaze unruffled, calm, serene.

A little lady, crabbed and brown,
And merging with the darkening street,
Sat staring as the sun sank down,
Oblivious of the stifling heat:
A picture of the living dead,
And framed with blossom, vibrant red.

DANCING GIRL

I saw her in a dream,
dancing barefoot
in a field of buttercups,
dark hair streaming, soft skirt swirling
white, as she leapt and twirled
with the laughing breeze
in the hazy morning light.

Where did she go —
the young girl in my dream,
dancing barefoot
in a field of buttercups?

WHAT AM I?

Full of days, my teeming brain
Peace has found in storm and strife,
Humbly giving, speaking plain
Words of wisdom, words of life.
  I am a sage, I clearly see;
  A guide and mentor. Learn from me.

Running tireless with the breeze,
Dark eyes laughing, bright with mirth,
Chasing rainbows, hugging trees,
Child of nature, child of earth.
  I am a gypsy, wild and free;
  A fiery spirit. Dance with me.

Loving life I leap and bound,
Scrape and scamper, romp and run,
Darting, dashing, twirling round,
Skipping, tripping, having fun.
  I am a kitten, full of glee;
  A ball of mischief. Play with me.

Churning passions rush and roar,
Restless, reckless, never still.
Deep and vast I plunge and soar,
Rough I threaten, roused I thrill.
  I am the vast, unfathomed sea;
  The mighty ocean. Rage with me.

Wide-eyed, trusting, free from doubt,
Asking questions, wondering why,
Loving, giving, reaching out,
Prone to giggles, quick to cry.
  I am a child, and want to be
  Just simply loved. Please care for me.

MADE IN HIS IMAGE

Made in his image, made to create,
Made to express from a knowledge innate
Of patterns and forms, new wonders of art,
New rhythms of music, new words from the heart,
To draft and design, to embellish and make
New objects of beauty for beauty's own sake.

Made in his image, made for concern,
To care for creation, to love and to learn
The deep hidden secrets of sky and the sea,
The land and its produce, each plant, every tree,
And all things that move, and to rightly observe,
And use with all wisdom, protect and preserve.

Made in his image, made to connect,
Relating to others with love and respect,
To seek understanding, to trust and believe,
To joyfully give and to humbly receive,
To share thoughts and feelings and gladly embrace
All peoples, all nations, each tribe, every race.

Made in his image, made to be me,
Living in fullness, unfettered and free,
To find my own shape and to know my own worth —
Unique, irreplaceable child of the earth —
To grow and develop in wisdom and love,
Enriched and empowered by my Father above.

O<>O<>O<>O<>O<>O<>O<>O

A child attempting
To imitate its Father:
The Creator God.

DAY 7

COMPLETION AND REST

Thus the heavens and the earth were completed in all their vast array,

By the seventh day God had finished the work he had been doing; so on the seventh day he rested from all his work. And God blessed the seventh day and made it holy, because on it he rested from all the work of creating that he had done. *(Genesis 2:1-3)*

GOD'S COMPLETE COMPLETION

God rested,
for creation was complete,
with nothing more to add
or take away.
Everything he saw was good,
everything was harmony,
everything as planned.

Not for God our incomplete completion.
We plan and organise our house –
our oikos: our environment –
expression of our human thought,
the labour of our hands.
We ponder, order, choose, reject;
we form and fashion, mould and make;
we look, admire, declare it good
and smile with pleasing pride.
Then slowly, soft, insidiously,
the doubts, the questions, start to rise;
they grow, expand, and fill our minds
with worrying unrest.

Such questions in our incomplete completion.
Have we got the balance right
of light and darkness, sunshine gold
and misty moonshine, pastel pearl,
or is it all too bright?
And was it such a good idea
to paint the ceiling azure blue?
Would pink be better, purple, plum,
or subtle silver grey?
And then those ruffled wavy rugs,
perhaps the texture's far too rough
to echo back the blue above
and blend with shades of earth.

Such doubting in our incomplete completion.
Is the carpet's deft design
of flowers and fauna, tree and fern
too complex for the human eye?
It should, perhaps, be plain.
And are the curtains hanging right:
those vapour drapings, soft as rain
and muted with the seasons' change,
are possibly too pale?
And then those fishes round the bath,
and eagle sculptures soaring high,
and wild-life paintings, photographs....
Oh, have I got it right?

No, not for God our incomplete completion.
God rested
for creation was complete,
with nothing more to add
or take away.
Everything he saw was good,
everything was harmony,
everything as planned.

IT IS FINISHED

It is finished.
God's creation
Is complete.
His love reached out
Across the world
And, after paradise,
He ordered rest.

It is finished.
God's redemption
Is complete.
His arms stretched out —
A cross his world —
And, through his sacrifice,
We enter rest.

WHAT IS REST?

A garden on a sunny day,
With winding paths and prospects fair,
Some butterflies in peaceful play,
A bird's song soaring, free of care,
And humming bees,
And shady trees
That gently fan the fragrant air.

A seashore and the shifting sand
Flushed warm beneath the smiling sun,
A sea breeze blowing soft inland,
And children playing, having fun,
And lapping waves
Around the caves
Where laughing streamlets leap and run.

A meadow wide, a sloping hill
With buttercups and daisies spread,
A lake with waters calm and still,
And white clouds floating, tinged with red,
The sun sunk low,
With holy glow
Anointing gold each drowsy head.

The curtains drawn against the night,
A cosy room with rustic charm,
A log fire spreading heat and light,
A constant heart, a loving arm
To strong enfold
And firmly hold,
Secure from every fear and harm.

GIFT OF REST

What have you done of worth today,
What thing accomplished? Tell me, pray.

I wandered down a country lane,
Enjoying warm the morning sun.
I lazed about, cast off the chain
Of mundane tasks and had some fun.
I met a friend, a favourite guest.
Today I gave my body rest.

What have you done of worth today,
What thing accomplished? Tell me, pray.

I sat and watched the flowers grow,
Took pleasure in their colours bright.
I smelled the breeze and felt it blow.
I gazed enthralled at dancing light
As soft the sun sank in the west.
Today my soul knew peace and rest.

What have you done of worth today,
What thing accomplished? Tell me, pray.

I let my thoughts go drifting free,
Indulged In dreams and, unconfined,
I soared to realms of fantasy
And left the world of work behind.
I used my Maker's last bequest.
Today my mind experienced rest.

A HOME

As sinks the sun in pale celestial beds,
The birds with glowing wings return to nest,
And in the treetops bow their sleepy heads,
Becalmed with thoughts of gentle night and rest.
The foxes too grow tired at last, and cold,
And leaving off the hunt seek out their lair;
While sheep lie snug and safe within the fold,
Protected by the shepherd's tender care.
And people blest, at end of weary day,
Put down their tools, shake off the strain and stress
Of working life, and wend their homeward way
To loving arms, and peace and quietness.
      For who has found a home, however base,
      Has found on this sad Earth a hallowed place.

RE-CREATION

What joy to leave dull toil and care,
To travel far and wide,
To breathe the sea or mountain air
And see the countryside;
Forgetting worry's pressing pain
And, leaving fear behind,
To feel new health and strength again,
And calming of the mind.

What joy to leave the madding crowds,
And clamour loud and rude,
To lie and watch the scudding clouds
In blessed solitude;
Forgetting turmoil, wrangling, strife,
Renewing faith and love,
Enjoying re-created life,
A taste of Heaven above.

HOLIDAYS

I sometimes wish that every day
Were like a summer holiday,
That every day the sun would shine,
And I could stay in bed till nine,
Then do what suited best my mood,
In company or solitude.
I'd walk or laze the whole day through,
And have no work at all to do.

I sometimes wish, when skies are grey,
That I could simply fly away
To some exotic sunny land
With mountains, valleys, sea and sand,
With palm trees growing by the shore,
And ancient ruins to explore,
And winding streets with houses white,
And market places, bustling, bright.

I sometimes wish that every day
I'd nothing else to do but play.
But really, if my dream came true
And skies were always clear and blue,
There'd be no purpose then in rest,
And pleasure would become a pest.
For when the long, cold winter's done,
It's then I welcome most the sun.

0<>0<>0<>0<>0<>0<>0<>0<>0

Fields of lavender
Wrapping the drowsy summer
In a purple mist.

BY QUIET WATERS

The sunlight sparkles on a stream
That winds around the silent hills;
A satin ribbon, gleaming bright,
And gently, gently flowing.

Beside the stream, in pastures green,
The cows, unruffled, peaceful graze.
With patient eyes they pensive stare
While softly, softly lowing.

The grassy fields are richly spread
With buttercups, in drifts of gold.
They lift their faces to the sky
While sweetly, sweetly growing.

The flowers are swaying in the breeze:
A kind, caressing zephyr warm
And fragrant with the scents of spring,
And calmly, calmly blowing.

The breeze is whispering words of cheer
As through the flowery fields I roam,
In Sabbath stillness rested, whole,
My soul restored and glowing.

O<>O<>O<>O<>O<>O<>O<>O

Pale yellow sunshine,
Clusters of primrose promise
Fallen from the sky.

SOUND OF LOVE

Rhythm of the pouring rain,
Heartbeat of the lowering sky,
Thrumming, drumming rapt refrain
The seasons round, a swishing sigh
Of sweet relief from Heaven above,
A pitter-patter sound of love.

Murmur of the gentle breeze,
Whisper of the balmy air,
Hushing, shushing calm the trees,
Soothing zephyr, fragrant, fair;
Breath of comfort, holy dove,
Soughing, sighing sound of love.

Rushing of the restless sea,
Waves upon the shingled shore,
Rattling, prattling, playful, free,
Pebbled chatter, hiss and roar
Of boisterous billows' push and shove,
A plashing, splashing sound of love.

Resonance of music, words,
Sound of silence — space and time;
Trilling, thrilling song of birds,
Rocks' and rivers' chant and chime,
Creature voices: treasure trove
Of God's creating, sound of love.

O<>O<>O<>O<>O<>O<>O<>O

In the beginning
Was the Word — the Logos — God.
And the Word was love.

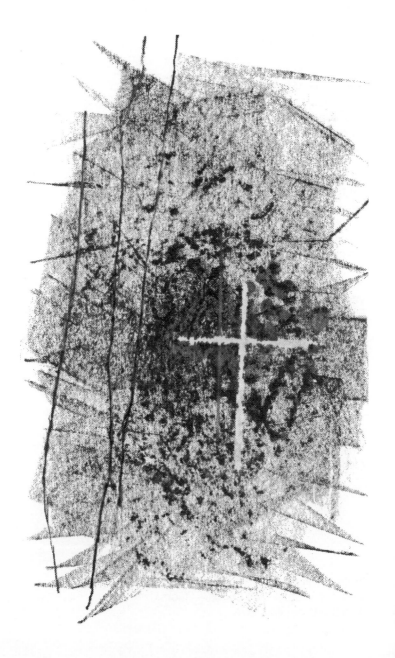

TODAY

CREATION ABUSED AND NEGLECTED

Woe to you who add house to house and join field to field till no space is left and you live alone in the land.

(Isaiah 5:8)

Hear the word of the LORD.... "There is no faithfulness, no love, no acknowledgment of God in the land. There is only cursing, lying and murder, stealing and adultery; they break all bounds, and bloodshed follows bloodshed. Because of this the land mourns, and all who live in it waste away; the beasts of the field and the birds of the air and the fish of the sea are dying." *(Hosea 4:1-3)*

MAN-MADE MONSTERS

A dragon in the sky,
formed from supersonic trails
and smoke from countless chimney stacks,
reaches to the stratosphere
and eats for breakfast
tender chunks of ozone,
which it kills with Its polluted breath;
and, basking in the burning sun,
it belches skin-destroying flame,
and pisses acid rain.

A serpent stalks the sea:
a sticky, stinking, oily slick
spawned from the blackest hell.
With appetite insatiable
it ruthlessly pursues its prey,
its viscid venom paralysing,
clinging, clogging, choking, killing,
devastating
sea and sand, the grass and trees,
and all that lives and moves and breathes.

A crazed wolf haunts the earth.
Wandering wildly to and fro,
it tears apart uranium
with gnashing, snarling neutron-teeth,
and buries in the hapless ground
its well-chewed bones: spent fuel rods
that falsely lie
till careless man or cruel nature
digs them up, releasing rabid poison
on an unsuspecting world.

FOREST ABUSE

Did the wind, exhausted now, bewail
The fallen forest he himself had slain
With such unwonted fury; flinging hail
Like one possessed — his freakish force insane —
And rooting up, with savage hands untamed,
The noble towers, violated, shamed?

And did he, shocked and trembling in the cold
Accusing light of day, now mourn the dead
As, rocked with guilt, he left a trail untold
Of cruel carnage: acres overspread
With severed limbs that, seeping life-blood, lay
With twisted trunks in grisly disarray?

And did his sister, rain, regret her part
In desecrating ancient woodlands green
As, not with overt rage, but cunning art
Developed over centuries unseen,
She poisoned with her bitterness the ground,
Creating offspring sickened, soured, unsound?

And did she, as her tears began to fall
Upon the silent acres, thudding fast
On fallen timber, angrily recall
The beat of her abuser — fiery blast
Of pounding, proud machines — till carbon-bruised
And broken, she, the victim, now abused?

O<>O<>O<>O<>O<>O<>O<>O<>O

Tree stumps — open tombs,
With torn limbs tossed and scattered
By the vandal wind.

TO A HEDGEHOG SQUASHED BY A CAR

0 hedgehog, squashed and bloody pelt
Abandoned in the road, where dwelt
You? Where's your leafy nest:
Your shield from world unrest?

And who laments your sudden end?
There must be someone, spouse or friend,
You've left bereft behind
Of suffering hedgehogkind.

And what enticed you to explore
The farther side, through reek and roar;
To risk your life and limb
In circumstances grim?

For rain or sunshine, night and day,
Unfeeling monsters pointless prey
On creatures weak, unwise,
Transfixing with their eyes.

Were you, then, hedgehog, terrified,
A Gorgo-victim petrified
Before those head lights bound,
While death with violent sound —

A brain-exploding, screeching squeal —
Flung you around his whirling wheel,
Spinning you, torn, until
He left you, limp and still?

Or did death take you unawares
While, bowed, you brooded on your cares,
Or dreamed a smiling dream:
Struck by a silent scream?

0 hedgehog, I can never know
What hopes and dreams you cherished so,
What cares you knew, what strife,
Your habits, way of life.

And so, although your violent mode
Of dying, lying in the road
So mangled, I regret,
I'll very soon forget.

For I've a journey hard ahead,
And cannot mourn for every dead
Unknown, or stop to cry.
Too many hedgehogs die.

EXTINCTION

Farmer, farmer, fell your trees,
Tear your hedgerows down.
Ensure that wildlife can't survive,
And earn God's angry frown.

Fisherman, go trawl your nets
Wider, deeper down.
Empty all the seas of fish,
And earn God's angry frown.

Hunter, hunter, seek your prey,
Ruthless track it down.
Destroy whole species in your greed,
And earn God's angry frown.

A CRYING NEED

The rain beat down upon a dingy street
Where houses huddled, small and strangely old;
And on a broken step, a shaky seat,
A little boy sat shivering in the cold.
With watchful eyes he stared into the night,
The windows of his soul thrown wide with fear.
But no one stopped. Oblivious of his plight,
They didn't see the single dirt-stained tear.
Nor did they see a body bent and bruised
By acts of violence — damaged human clay
Grown old too soon as, battered and bemused,
He sat and mourned another dying day.
      Oh, shameful loss! A tragedy indeed
      When life creates such crying, unmet need.

The smiling sun shone warmly on a glade
Of summer flowers, where stood a mansion fair;
And on the grass, a child contented played,
Her face serene, and seeming free from care.
And no one knew that, lost in happy dreams,
The child escaped a secret life of shame:
The nightly visits, pain and muffled screams;
The menaced threats, confusion, guilt and blame.
And no one saw, beyond the prosperous ground,
Her inner bleakness. So, she dwelt alone,
Inventing richly worlds in which she found
The love that in real life she'd never known.
      Oh, sad reality! A crime indeed
      When life creates such crying, unmet need.

PROPAGANDA

A soldier lies
upon the screen sand,
dead,
his waxy face half hidden
in the heated grains,
his body posed:
a model dressed
in faded camouflage
artistically arranged
to advertise the allies' strength,
their smug supremacy,
and ridicule with cold compare
the rival companies' claim.

And as he lies,
the soldier on the screen sand
dead,
unreal, unrecognised,
somewhere a mother howls.

0<>0<>0<>0<>0<>0<>0<>0

A thing of beauty,
The joy of generations,
Lying in ruins.
Can a bridge be built again
That was torn apart by war?

GOD, WHAT ARE WE DOING TO YOUR WORLD?

Oh, God, what are we doing
to your world?
Like children with a picture book,
we scribble over works of art
and think they are improved.

And oftentimes we grab
your picture world
with grubby hands, not caring if
we smudge and smear each pristine page
with dirt indelible.

And greedy-eyed, we want to view
your world —
each page, each picture — all at once,
and in our haste to have it all
we tear it, leaf by leaf.

And God, we even fight about
your world.
And in our childish tugs-of-war
we wrench the pages from the spine
that binds — then think we've won!

We haven't learned to value, yet,
your world.
Like children, God, we damage it,
then leave it, when we fall asleep,
for some adult to mend.

0<>0<>0<>0<>0<>0<>0<>0

Rows of brick boxes
For packing up the beauty
Of ancient meadows.

NEW CREATION

A tale is told through ages long
In myths and dreams, an ancient song
Revealed in time, now written plain:
A God who dies and lives again,
A God come down to sinful Earth
To bring redemption, second birth.

And through his resurrection might
A brand new world of glorious light,

While living water, pure and sweet,
Flows fresh from wounded hands and feet;

The woods rejoice, and fields divine
Bring forth new produce, corn and wine

As, soaring through the heavens above,
The sun rekindled beams its love;

And fish that swim and birds that fly
Replenish rivers, sea and sky,

And creatures rise, the great and small,
With man restored from Adam's Fall.

For God so loved, he gave his Son —
The one of three, the three in one —
Come down to Earth in human clay;
A dying seed, a new spring day
To banish winter harsh and long
And fill the world once more with song:

The song of the redeemed and blest
Who enter his eternal rest.

Index of Poems

Untitled poems (Japanese haiku and tanka) are listed by first lines and shown in italics.

JENNIFER MINNEY graduated from Bible College with Distinction, after which she spent six years in full-time Christian ministry before training as a nurse and midwife.

She and her husband moved to Germany in 1979, where she graduated from the University of Maryland (European Division) with a BA (Summa cum Laude) in Psychology, with English Literature and Writing as her minor subject. As the top graduate in Europe, she was the winner of the university's Colonel Bentley Award.

Whilst in Germany, Jennifer trained and worked as a counsellor for the US Forces. Since her return to England in 1994, she has worked as a GP-based counsellor for the NHS, and has established a thriving private practice.

Jennifer was first published nationally at age seventeen, and has since had works published in Britain and the US. Her interest in creativity and the creative process is an underlying theme in some of her other books, in particular *Self-esteem: the way of humility*, in which readers are helped to discover and enhance their own creative potential.

In all her books, Jennifer draws on her varied training and experience, as well as her writing skills, to produce books that are noted for their depth, freshness and originality. They are a valuable resource for anyone seeking spiritual and emotional fulfilment.

RAY CATTELL moved from Britain to Canada in the 1950s and has become a leading figure in Canadian painting. He has won many coveted prizes and his works are found in major public and private collections, including the Royal Collection at Windsor Castle. He is a member of the Royal Canadian Academy of Arts and a past president of the Canadian Society of Painters in Watercolour.

Also by Jennifer Minney

Self-esteem: The way of humility

The author draws on her long experience of counselling people with damaged self-esteem, together with biblical teaching and the findings of psychological research, to examine self-development in the larger context of our identity in God and our role as stewards of creation.

The book also explores self-identity as it is shaped by our socio-political, cultural, ecclesiastical, family and personal history. It discusses the causes and effects of low self-esteem, and looks at ways of improving every aspect of the self—social, mental, physical, emotional and spiritual—whilst also focusing on the need to rediscover our connectedness with God and the entire created world.

The book is divided into easily-readable sections, and has sixteen line drawings. It contains a comprehensive index, a bibliography, exercises and questionnaires. It will be a help, not only to people struggling with this very common problem, but also to ministers, group leaders, counsellors and students.

"She looks at how we see ourselves, our needs of love and acceptance, our creativity and innate curiosity, the relationships between body, mind and soul…. How the omnipresent Creator God made us in His image to be individually creative. This book is easy to read and free of jargon. I commend it."
The Association of Christian Counsellors

£5.95   **ISBN: 0-9538446-2-5**

The Grobook Series

Jennifer Minney, an experienced counsellor, SRN and SCM, with a BA (Summa cum Laude) in Psychology and a Bible College Diploma with Distinction, has combined medical and psychological knowledge with biblical truths to produce a series of books on some common emotional problems that hinder personal growth and development.

Using Biblical characters as case studies, each book discusses causes, signs and symptoms, and gives practical suggestions for overcoming the immediate effects. The reader is also helped to understand and change dysfunctional patterns of thinking and behaviour: to move beyond the problem towards spiritual and psychological wholeness.

Beyond depression: Growing into light
"The author has used her technical knowledge and experience to produce a well-rounded guide on the subject. It does not talk down to the reader, nor does language form a barrier."
ISBN: 0-9538446-3-3

Beyond fear: Growing into faith
"Good basic information. These books could help hurting people."   **ISBN: 0-9538446-5-X**

Beyond stress: Growing into serenity
"Presented clearly and practically. Simple to understand and devoid of waffle… For me this is value."
ISBN: 0-9538446-4-1

Reviews by The Association of Christian Counsellors

£3.50 each

Will Jesus kick my ball back?

"He will probably never walk, or use any of his right side. He might also be mentally retarded. And he'll probably be epileptic. If I were you, I would put him in a home and forget him."

This is the amazing story of an adoption that should have been impossible, and of an endearing, giggly child whom a neurologist had written off. It is also the story of the author's spiritual and psychological journey, from a background of abuse and rejection to a place of trust in God's goodness.

The book gives no simplistic answers to life's problems, but encourages readers to reflect and enlarge their concept of God, so that they can trust him in all circumstances.

"In this book there is a real sense that God knew what Jonathan needed most, and He has provided. What they achieved has been born out of such a depth of love. To say more than that in this review would spoil the read of the book!"
The Association of Christian Counsellors

£6.95   **ISBN: 0-9538446-0-9**

Living through Grief

Although everyone's grief is different, there are recognised phases, each with its own set of fluctuating emotions. The author explains the grief process and gently leads the reader through each of the stages, from the first shock and disbelief to healing and recovery, This book has something for everyone — comfort, reassurance, practical guidance and, above all, hope.

"Delivers professional advice in an accessible and positive way. Informative and helpful, in no way presumptuous or patronising… with a broad readability and distilled experience."
The Association of Christian Counsellors

£2.50   **ISBN: 0-9538446-6-8**

All Silvertree titles are available from bookshops or can be purchased (postage free in UK) direct from:

Silvertree Publishing
PO Box 2768
Yeovil
Somerset
BA22 8XZ

Become a Silvertree Book Agent

If you found this book helpful, why not become a Silvertree Book Agent, and so benefit others whilst also earning money for yourself, your church, or your favourite charity?

For full details, send an s.a.e. to the above address.